SYMBOLS

of the

Nativity

~○ JEANA JAMES ○~

CFI
An Imprint of Cedar Fort, Inc.
Springville, Utah

ISBN 13: 978-1-4621-1659-1

Published by CFI, an imprint of Cedar Fort, Inc.
2373 W. 700 S., Springville, UT 84663
Distributed by Cedar Fort, Inc., www.cedarfort.com

LIBRARY OF CONGRESS CATALOGING-IN-PUBLICATION DATA

James, Jeana, 1966- author.
   Symbols of the nativity / Jeana James.
      pages cm
   Includes bibliographical references and index.
   ISBN 978-1-4621-1659-1 (alk. paper)
   1. Crèches (Nativity scenes) I. Title.

GT4989.5.J35 2015
394.2663--dc23

                              2015023855

Cover design by Shawnda T. Craig
Cover design © 2015 Lyle Mortimer
Edited and typeset by Kevin Haws

Printed in the United States of America

10 9 8 7 6 5 4 3 2 1

Printed on acid-free paper

ne tradition many Christian families share is the display of the beautiful Nativity scene each Christmas season. Historically, the Nativity is a single group depicting, in a simple visual display, the beauty and power of the birth of Christ. Though it is and has been displayed in many ways throughout history and the world, the sublime meaning is the same. The Nativity reminds us of the miracle of the birth of our Savior and the significance of His ministry in our own lives. The simpleness of the scene brings warm feelings of love, peace, joy, and gratitude. The presence of the Nativity helps us to center our focus on the true meaning of Christmas and the greatest gift given to mankind.

But have you ever paused to think about the pieces of the Nativity and what meaning each one may symbolize in your own life?

Stable

When you set out the stable in your scene, think of it representing your heavenly and earthly parents. Heavenly Father gives us many shelters to help protect us and bring happiness, peace, and joy to our lives. But we must choose to take cover, letting his love surround, protect, and comfort us. Following the teachings of Jesus Christ gives us refuge from our wearisome world.

Earthly parents likewise shelter and protect. They love and nurture us until we are able to withstand the harsh elements often found in the world. Though they cannot always keep out all of the cold and harshness, they do their best because they love us. Loving parents are a great gift from God.

Luke 2:7

And she brought forth her firstborn son, and wrapped him in swaddling clothes, and laid him in a manger; because there was no room for them in the inn.

Angel

Next, place the angel in your scene. The Lord sent an angel messenger to announce the glorious event, linking earth and heaven in a divine way. Angels minister, protect, and deliver God's messages. They bring peace and comfort, surrounding us especially during times of need. Realize that the angel in the Nativity represents all of us, since we each rejoiced with incredible gladness on the night our Savior was born. We had waited, longing for the day because we knew it was the first step in unlocking the doors to allow us to have the gifts of eternal blessings and everlasting life. The celebration that took place in heaven must have been a joy beyond anything we have ever seen or felt on this earth.

Luke 2:10, 13–14

And the angel said unto them, Fear not: for, behold, I bring you good tidings of great joy, which shall be to all people. . . . And suddenly there was with the angel a multitude of the heavenly host praising God, and saying, Glory to God in the highest, and on earth peace, good will toward men.

Donkey

Add the donkey next. The donkey plays a significant part in the Nativity scene. Known for steadiness and strength, the donkey carried the burden of Mary, making the trip to Bethlehem for the birth of Christ easier for her. Are we like the donkey? Are we willing to carry the burdens of others and help them on their way? The Savior asks this of us because this is what He has done for us. Recommit today, and always, to unselfishly serve and help others, for this is where you find the true spirit of Christ and Christmas.

Luke 2:30–32

For mine eyes have seen thy salvation, which thou hast prepared before the face of all people; a light to lighten the Gentiles, and the glory of thy people Israel.

Animals

The stable animals are the next pieces to add to your Nativity. The animals witnessed the birth of the Son of God in the stable that first Christmas night. They are an important part of the Nativity because they created a humble scene as they shared the beautiful night with the others who were present. Jehovah's creatures knew that the Child was indeed the Son of God; oftentimes His own people did not. The animals brought a sincere reverence to the scene as they shared their manger with Mary, Joseph, and the Newborn King.

We, at times, may not fully appreciate our shelter or those who surround us. We may even wonder why we are sharing the same shelter with them. But keep in mind, as Mary and Joseph did that first Christmas night, it is far better to have cover and be in with the animals than out in the cold alone.

Luke 2:12

And this shall be a sign unto you; Ye shall find the babe wrapped in swaddling clothes, lying in a manger.

Isaiah 1:3

The ox knoweth his owner, and the ass his master's crib: but Israel doth not know, my people doth not consider.

Shepherds

Now add the shepherds to your scene. Imagine yourself as one of the shepherds as they carefully watched over and cared for the fold. Have you wondered why the angel delivered the good tidings to the shepherds? Perhaps it was symbolic of the Savior's mission—the Shepherd, leading us safely back home. We, like Jesus Christ and the shepherds, have been asked to watch over and care for each other.

Think of how the shepherds must have felt when the angel suddenly appeared to tell them of the miraculous event. Reflect on their feelings as they tried to comprehend what was being announced. Imagine their overwhelming joy and excitement as they followed the star to the baby Jesus that first Christmas. Like the shepherds, if we follow the light of Christ, it will lead us to Him and to eternal life. Stay true to the light, and you will always know where you should go and what you should do.

Luke 2:8–10, 15–16

And there were in the same country shepherds abiding in the field, keeping watch over their flock by night. And, lo, the angel of the Lord came upon them. . . . And the angel said unto them, Fear not: for, behold, I bring you good tidings of great joy, which shall be to all people. . . . And it came to pass, as the angels were gone away from them into heaven, the shepherds said one to another, Let us now go even unto Bethlehem, and see this thing which is come to pass, which the Lord hath made known unto us. And they came with haste, and found Mary, and Joseph, and the babe lying in a manger.

Camel

Next, add the camel. Known for strength and endurance, the camel escorted the wise men to witness the Child. The camel reminds us that we should set our sights on an unwavering journey, being strong and steadfast and living in a way that will one day allow us to kneel at the Savior's feet. As we set our sights with an eye single to God, we will arrive where we want to be: in the presence of our God and Savior.

Matthew 1:21

And she shall bring forth a son, and thou shalt call his name Jesus: for he shall save his people from their sins.

First Wise Man

As you add the first wise man to your Nativity, realize that these were no ordinary men. They were on an errand to witness the arrival of the Son of God on the earth. Their righteousness was evident because they could see the star when others could not. The wise men were witnesses of the Christ Child. God has proclaimed that through two or more witnesses we shall know truth. The wise men traveled far to witness the beautiful sight of the Child. Maybe, at times, they wanted to give up their journey, but they knew what a blessed experience it would be to lay their eyes upon the Newborn King. They longed to pour out their love and respect to the Son of God. Our life is like the wise men's journey. It will be long and hard at times but worth it in the end, when we are able to be with our Savior forever. If we open our hearts to Him, He will dwell within us and guide and direct us.

Matthew 2:1–2

Now when Jesus was born in Bethlehem of Judaea in the days of Herod the king, behold, there came wise men from the east to Jerusalem, saying, Where is he that is born King of the Jews? For we have seen his star in the east, and are come to worship him.

Second Wise Man

As you place the second wise man, think of this: The wise men brought many precious gifts to the baby Jesus. The elegant gifts of gold, frankincense, and myrrh were given with great respect, devotion, and humility to the Child. Traditional Christmas gift exchanges today have reference to the gifts presented by the wise men to Jesus. And even today, we have the opportunity to give gifts to Christ, as the wise men of old did—by keeping His commandments, serving others, and always remembering Him. Truly striving to be like Him is all He asks of us, that His sacrifice be not in vain.

Matthew 2:10–11

When they saw the star, they rejoiced with exceeding great joy. And when they were come into the house, they saw the young child with Mary his mother, and fell down, and worshipped him: and when they had opened their treasures, they presented unto him gifts; gold, and frankincense, and myrrh.

Third Wise Man

Remember, as you set out the third wise man, that the many gifts the wise men brought to the baby Jesus that first Christmas night do not compare with what He has given to each of us. Gift-giving by Saint Nicholas symbolizes the unconditional gift given by Jesus Christ to all Heavenly Father's children. Through His life on this earth, His death, and His Resurrection, He has given us the greatest gift of all, that of everlasting life. This gift is given to all mankind through a love so pure that we cannot even begin to comprehend it. Even today, wise men seek after Him. Will you be wise and allow Him to direct your life and perfect you?

Matthew 2:9

When they had heard the king, they departed; and, lo, the star, which they saw in the east, went before them, till it came and stood over where the young child was.

Joseph

Now add Joseph to your Nativity scene. Think of the significance of the humble Joseph. Imagine how he must have felt when a messenger of God told him of his calling to be the earthly father of the Savior. Do you think he felt prepared, worthy, or even willing to take on what would lie ahead for him? I am sure it was a humbling and refining season for him, as the Lord prepared him for his earthly mission. We too must humble ourselves and be prepared to accept the callings and obligations God has given to us on this earth, because none of us know what may be expected of us. Are we ready?

Matthew 1:20, 24

But while he thought on these things, behold, the angel of the Lord appeared unto him in a dream, saying, Joseph, thou son of David, fear not to take unto thee Mary thy wife: for that which is conceived in her is of the Holy Ghost. . . . Then Joseph being raised from sleep did as the angel of the Lord had bidden him, and took unto him his wife.

Mary

Think of the precious Mary as you add her to your scene. Mary was highly favored of God because of her righteousness, goodness, and purity. She is a beautiful daughter of God and an exquisite example of motherhood. The gift of the Living Son of God whom Mary gave to each of us is beyond measure.

Think of the great blessing each of us has when we hold our own children in our arms. Think of the joy we feel each time a new baby is born into our families. It must have been much the same for Mary on the first Christmas night. As daughters and sons of God, we have the opportunity of experiencing a glimpse of what Mary felt. We have the blessing of knowing and feeling in our hearts a part of the endless love God truly has for each of His precious children.

Luke 1:28, 30–31

And the angel came in unto her, and said, Hail, thou that art highly favoured, the Lord is with thee: blessed art thou among women. . . . And the angel said unto her, Fear not, Mary: for thou hast found favour with God. And, behold, thou shalt conceive in thy womb, and bring forth a son, and shalt call his name Jesus.

Luke 2:19

But Mary kept all these things, and pondered them in her heart.

Baby Jesus

Last, add the most important piece of all to the Nativity: the baby Jesus! He is the most significant because His birth is the center of the beautiful Nativity and of our salvation. Strive to have Him be the center of Christmas and your life.

We must always remember that He is the reason for the season. He is the Light of the World. As we choose to follow Him, we shall not walk in darkness, but shall have His guiding light to lead us to everlasting life. He will fill our lives with peace, joy, and happiness. He will guide us home. Commit today and every day to know the Light of Christ and share the Light of Christ with the world.

Matthew 1:23

Behold, a virgin shall be with child, and shall bring forth a son, and they shall call his name Emmanuel, which being interpreted is, God with us.

Luke 2:11, 14

For unto you is born this day in the city of David a Saviour, which is Christ the Lord. . . . Glory to God in the highest, and on earth peace, good will toward men.

et us always remember the eternal significance and importance of putting Jesus Christ at the center of not only Christmas but also our entire lives!

Luke 2:40

And the child grew, and waxed strong in spirit, filled with wisdom: and the grace of God was upon him.

0 26575 16591 3